# THE KIDS' SOLAR ENERGY BOOK

# THE KIDS' SOLAR ENERGY BOOK

## EVEN GROWN-UPS CAN UNDERSTAND

by Tilly Spetgang and Malcolm Wells

imagine!
Publishing

Copyright © 1982, 2009 by Tilly Spetgang, Malcolm Wells and Solar Service Corporation

An Imagine Book
Published by Charlesbridge
85 Main Street
Watertown, MA 02472
617-926-0329
www.charlesbridge.com

ISBN-13: 978-1-936140-46-6
Library of Congress Control Number: 2011924324

Designed by Marc Cheshire

Printed and manufactured in China, June 2013
10 9 8 7 6 5 4 3 2

# Contents

# Foreword

Twenty-seven years ago they were friends: Malcolm Wells (an architect), Irwin Spetgang (an engineer) and his wife, Tilly (a journalist). They shared a *strong* belief in trying to save this beautiful blue-green planet of ours.

Out of that grew this book. Mac is an artist with a wild sense of humor; he let loose, and the other two jumped in with creative chips. They turned to

Malcolm Wells as a boy.

Tilly for a crystal-clear story of solar . . . and how it works.

But that was in 1982. The world wasn't listening. Few had even heard of global warming and diminishing drinkable water. Now it's on the cover of *Time* and an essential item on our President's agenda.

So here's a brand-new version of *The Kids' Solar Energy Book* even grown-ups can understand. It's aimed at kids (it will be *their* world in a flash) and the people who love them.

Malcolm Wells and "company" had a blast creating this book. Hope you enjoy . . . and laugh, and learn.

# Injustice, Hunger, and Your Glorious Future

This world is yours.

This beautiful blue-green planet of mountains and oceans and skyscrapers and great beasts of the jungles. . . . all yours.

Have you ever thought about it that way?

You may be about 12 years old and not feel as if you count in any special way outside your family.

But, in the wink of an eye, you will be 18, 23, 32.

Then you will be in the position of electing the politicians who make the rules of the land.

I'm already 18-23-32 and I wouldn't recommend it to anyone.

Oh, wow.

You may own property, pay taxes, and help decide how that tax money should be spent.

You will have power!

As you grow older, you will begin to realize how many cruel and unjust things go on in life.

You probably will try to change some of these injustices.

I found that out in first grade . . . during recess.

Not anymore, I won't. With all my power nobody will mess with me.

It may be that people are hungry and are not being fed. You may fight to stop the killing of giant whales, the clubbing of baby seals.

You may come to feel that the spread of nuclear power means deadly destruction.

"Fight to stop the killing!"
That can be our motto.

"Kill to kill
the killing!"

"Kill to stop
the fighting!"

Or, if my paycheck comes from the power company, I may come to feel that a meltdown or two is a small price to pay for energy independence.

As an adult, you will be able to give your time, your creative efforts, and your money to help solve some of the world's problems.

One of the most serious of those problems that *you* will have to deal with will be . . . energy.

You've heard about the energy crunch.

Your mother lowers the temperature in the house . . . to save energy.

Yeah. It's a new candy bar.

I thought it was when two oil tankers collided.

Are you <u>kidding</u>? <u>My</u> mother keeps it set a 75°, day and night.

Your father carpools with two other people . . . to save energy.

You are asked to turn off lights and the television when you leave the room . . . to save energy.

Why do we *have* to save energy?

Why can't we simply fill the gas tank in the car, the oil tank in the basement, or flip a switch so we have electricity whenever we want it? What's all the noise about, anyway?

Well, to be truthful, most people want to save energy because it costs so much.

But the major underlying problem is oil.

We're running out of it.

It takes an enormously long time for oil to be created in the earth, where heat and pressure help to form it.

Good. That'll get rid of the oil problem.

Yes. it's much better to make it in refineries where it takes only a few days.

The oil we've pumped out in the past ten years may have taken millions of years to form.

You can plainly see that we cannot keep using oil this recklessly or it will be gone in the future, when you, and your children, will need it. Oil is very important.

It is used to make plastics and medicine, for instance.

It keeps giant machinery running.

In the form of gas it makes cars move, it is important to farming because fertilizer is made from it, and it helps make electricity.

All over the world right now, methods are being studied of creating energy without depending on oil.

Fertilizer helps make electricity? Too bad Ben Franklin didn't know that.

Dummy. She means farming helps make electricity.

Obviously, whoever is studying them never studied the first law of thermodynamics: "energy can neither be created nor destroyed".

One of those ways is to use solar energy . . . using the sun for heat.

# How It All Began

If you stopped a caveman and asked him (assuming there was a language you both spoke) where he learned about passive solar heating, he wouldn't know what you were talking about.

I think that's a pretty safe assumption.

cavemen: STOP here!

But the caveman used the sun in a smart manner. He moved into caves facing south, from where the sun shines.

Hey, that really was smart of him.

I wish Ronald would stop making those bug noises.

This gave him sunlight, which baked the floor and walls of his stone cave during a good part of the day. Then, at nightfall, when the weather turned cold, those walls and floor gave back much of the same heat, warming the caveman and his family.

In America's very early days, the Pueblo Indians built their adobe rooms into the south face of cliffs. They used the sun exactly the way cave dwellers did . . . for stored heat in walls and floor.

How did they know about it?

Simple. They must have felt with their hands how the stone sucked up heat during the day and then released it at night.

Maybe they were students of yours.

Or maybe it was just warmer that way.

Maybe they knew Al Gore.

No. I think history tells us they always felt stone with their elbows.

They were smart people, and they applied what they knew to their dwellings.

In a major exposition (like a world's fair) in France during the late 1890s, one of the most exciting exhibits showed how a piece of machinery could be run by the sun.

And that's how wallpaper was invented?

I thought you said it was oil that made machinery run. Come on, now, you can't have it both ways.

A shiny metal parabola (nothing more than a large, curved dish) focused the sun's rays on a black tank of water. When the water in the tank boiled, it gave off steam.

The steam was sent through a pipe to run a small steam engine, which, in turn, was the driving power for a printing press.

As water will often do when boiled.

Printing press! What happened to that piece of machinery we were just discussing? OK. Never mind. I get it now. Then what happened?

The press printed leaflets . . .

which explained that all the work of printing the leaflet had been done by the sun—without electricity or other power sources.

It was, and still is, a great source of wonder.

Also, in the late 1890s, in the southern parts of the United States, several types of solar systems were sold to people in Florida and California.

These were roof mounted solar collectors that heated water used for dishwashing, baths, and laundry.

Heating water by using the sun's rays was a great deal easier for people living in those hot southern states than chopping wood, building a fire, and keeping a stove going in the heat of the summer.

So solar energy was very popular then.

But in the early 1900s, oil and gas were discovered (the very fuels that are becoming scarce now).

Then the oil problem arrived, I'll bet.

What'd I tell you?

People quickly learned that all they had to do was run gas through a pipe, then light the gas as it came out.

It was cheap. It was easy. Solar energy was put aside as being too bothersome.

And much less fun.

But in the late 1950s, rumblings were heard about possible fuel shortages.

Most people pooh-poohed the rumors because the idea was so strange.

Hadn't there always been plenty of oil and gas?

Wouldn't they continue . . . forever?

No! They were discovered only sixty years earlier, remember? You told us yourself.

We can't wait to find out.

But a few people around the country listened very carefully.

Rumble-checkers, they were called.

They were known as conservationists. They began to change their lifestyles so they would use less electricity, water, coal, gas, and oil.

Why use less of all those things if only oil and gas were the subjects of the rumblings?

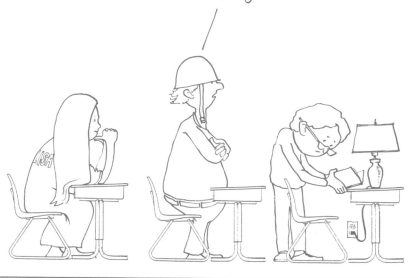

And out of their searching for ways of saving fuels grew a renewed interest in solar energy.

These early conservationists studied, experimented (one woman in Princeton placed homemade solar panels on her garage roof that heated the oven in her house, enabling her to cook and bake by the sun's free heat), and began to put their money and thoughts into solar energy.

Today there are many good manufacturers of solar energy systems and many fine engineers and architects who are able to design solar systems properly.

Industry, as well as government, is studying solar energy seriously as a way to stop depending on foreign oil.

(And just one or two unscrupulous bums out to milk the industry for all it's worth.)

FOREIGN oil? Isn't the whole world running out, or is it just us?

You will benefit from all this solar activity. And some day, when you are an adult, you may remember learning your solar energy basics. Enjoy.

# Active Solar Systems

Energy from the sun is free and always available.

It doesn't pollute the air as oil and coal do.

But there's a catch, right? You have to do something expensive in order to use it.

Boy, was I misinformed! I thought it was only the products of their combustion that polluted the air.

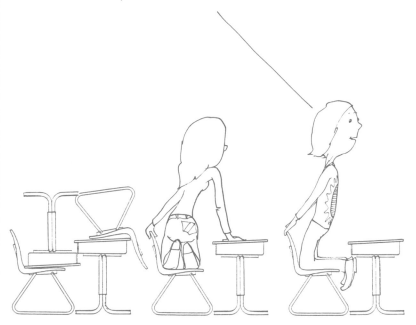

It's a natural way of heating air and water. So you may wonder why *everybody* doesn't use solar energy instead of oil.

Well, in some countries, everybody *does*.

In Israel and Japan, for instance, solar panels dot roofs everywhere.

That's because those countries have no oil or coal of their own and must buy energy from other countries at very high prices. America is rich in coal, but still imports more than half the oil it uses. It needs solar energy to reduce its dependence on oil imports.

Another reason everybody doesn't use solar energy instead of oil is that it's a fairly new idea.

People don't quite know how it works and arc a bit nervous about anything they don't understand. But in *your* world . . . the near tomorrow . . . there will be many, many more solar buildings.

Your home will probably use solar energy. So you should know and understand what it is and how it works.

Have you learned that the sun is a star, the same kind of star you see crowding the heavens on a dark night?

It is a light, heat, and energy star composed of burning gases.

The sun is the star nearest to the earth, which turns about it, gathering up heat and light from this flaming neighbor 93,000,000 miles away.

Funny, I always thought it was more of a thermonuclear reaction brought about by the crushing forces of its immense gravitational field.

This stuff is too complicated for me.

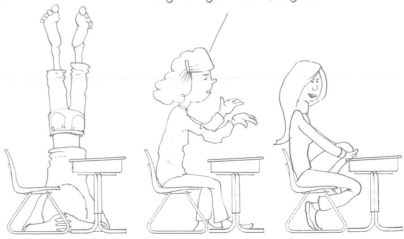

So what's the problem if we're getting all this heat? Ah, I get it: the heat is only good for running printing presses and baking bread on garage roofs, right?

So there is the sun, giving its heat away free. But this is the problem: How do you catch sunbeams to make them work for you?

One way is through the use of a solar collector, which is nothing more than a different way of saying sun collector; it collects the sun's heat.

It does it the way a greenhouse works.

A greenhouse is made mostly of glass to catch hot sunshine through its roof so flowers, plants, and vegetables can grow in it all through the bitter winter months.

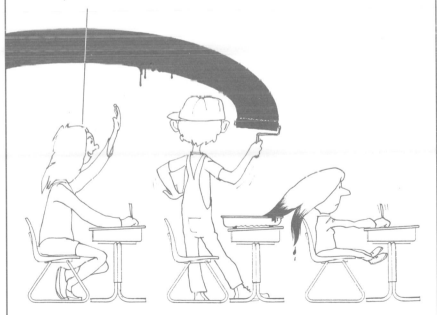

You fill the solar collector with plants and flowers?

Doesn't a greenhouse use more fuel than almost any other type of building? Or are you talking about a solar greenhouse, the kind that uses no energy but sunlight?

A solar collector is usually a flat box that lies on the roof of the house.

The box can be made of metal with a glass cover, just like a little flat greenhouse. But, when the sun comes through the glass and hits the inside of the box, it stops being sunlight and turns into heat. The inside of the box, which is black, gets very hot. It stays hot until water in special pipes flows over it to cool it off.

Air can cool it, too.

The heat is now in the water (or in the air, if you used air, but let's talk about water).

The hot water flows into a tank where it is stored.

Then, when the house gets cool and heat is needed, a fan blows air past the hot water tank.

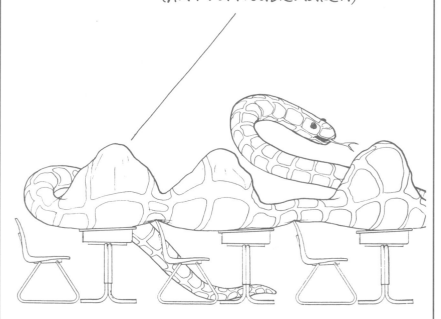

This warms the air, which then flows all through the house, eventually coming out through the grille in your bedroom.

# Passive Solar Systems

So there we have it: the collection, transformation, and use of energy. The energy which traveled to earth only a few hours earlier as sunlight is now warming my bod. What happens next? Does the energy simply disappear? Or do I release it as heat through my breath and sweat?

Tune in later and find out.

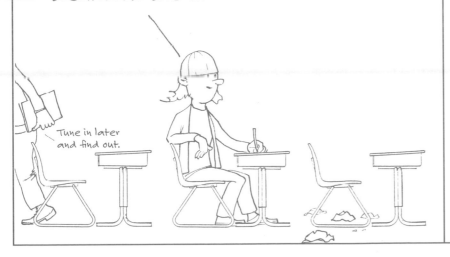

The solar collector you've just read about is part of an "active" solar system because it is made up of moving parts, such as fans and pumps, which need electricity to power them.

There is another solar energy system that is growing very popular with people who are interested in using the sun's energy. It is called a "passive" solar system because it has no moving parts.

And we're not telling how the electricity is made, are we? (Ain't I just awful?)

Don't you consider the billions of racing electronic particles "moving parts"?

In a passive solar system, the sun heats part of the house or "something" that holds the heat, then releases it when needed. That "something" can be an inside wall made of cement, brick, or stone, called a Trombe wall. Or the "something" could be barrels of water, or a bin filled with rocks.

You know how you enjoy running barefoot in the summer and how, if you run out into the street, it can burn the bottoms of your feet—it's so hot.

Will you please make up your mind?

Passive solar energy burns your feet?

Even at night, long after the sun has gone down, the street is still warm to your feet.

Well, that's how passive solar energy works.

It was stupid of me to keep standing out there all day.

I knew it. It's a foot-burner.

The street catches the sun, holds it all day and even through the night.

So build your house in the middle of the street and you'll never need oil again. Right?

Some new houses are being built with twice as many windows facing south as towards the north. The reason?

Let me guess: to run the printing presses?

The sun shines from the south, and this gives a house the chance to "collect" the warmth—the same way a solar collector collects sunlight.

Just like a little flat greenhouse. I remember.

Some people are building greenhouses on the south side of their homes.

Then shouldn't the greenhouses be called green<u>homes</u>?

That way, the greenhouse collects the sun all day, storing its warmth in water containers or in rocks. This very heat warms the house when it gets cold.

Another kind of passive system is to have water-filled tall plastic columns behind windows of a house to absorb the sun's heat.

Also, instead of having a stone or cement wall standing upright, a concrete floor (which is like a wall, only it's lying down) . . .

can serve as a collector of sun scooped up by south-facing windows.

It's really simple to make the sun work for you. All you have to do is open the room to sunshine through windows.

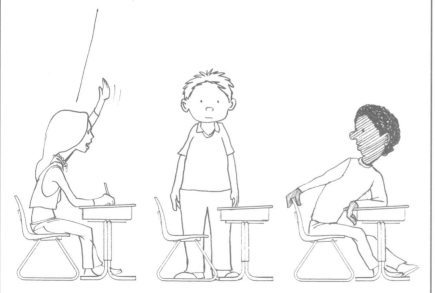

Sounds like quite a house, with walls lying on the floor and plastic water tanks all over the place.

And knock over a few walls.

Then, when the sun goes down, close off the windows with heavy shades, drapes, or indoor shutters. That way you trap the sun's heat in the room.

Some good points about "active" solar heat are:
1. It is easier to control the amount of heat you get and where it goes
2. It can be added to houses that are already built, much more easily than "passive"
3. There are many solar companies that understand and can install active systems.

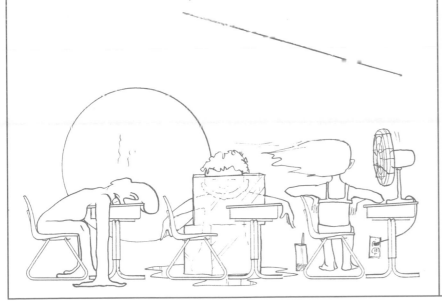

Some good points about "passive" solar heat are:
1. It uses no electricity
2. It often uses parts of the house (such as walls or the floor) to store warmth
3. It doesn't need as much care as an active system.

That's nice.

# Insulation

Neither of the two systems, active or passive, will do a house much good if the house is not insulated.

Is that a new word for you?

It means putting a blanket between the house and the outside, keeping the heat on one side, the cold on the other. There are many ways of accomplishing that.

Perhaps you've seen television commercials about insulating the attic, where a man is seen laying down material on the floor of the attic.

And we are about to hear of them, I suspect.

Is he about to make a new dress?

That is an excellent way to keep the house's heat in the house, where it belongs, instead of in the attic, where nobody lives.

Insulation is any material that traps air and does not permit heat to pass through easily. It could be cork, paper, different types of plastics that have bubbles caught in them, sponge, rock-wool, glass-wool, fiberglass, or other products.

Except for that poor dressmaker up there.

Or balloons?

How about soapsuds?

Air itself is insulation, probably the best, and we know that wool (wool winter coat, wool sweater) is an insulator because it does not allow your body heat to escape.

There are many places in a home that need insulation.

And we're going to stuff each one with a wool sweater.

It might be a good idea if you went around your own home and checked off the following:

1. Do you feel air leaking in around windows and doors?

2. Does snow on your roof melt more quickly than on the roofs of neighboring houses? (That's because the heat in your house is escaping through the ceiling and the roof, and melting the snow.)

3. Is the hot water heater in your basement covered with insulation? If it isn't, some of the heat escapes into the basement, where it is wasted.

I can't tell what that big wooly lump is down there.

4. Are drapes closed and shades pulled when the sun goes down?

No, we have to do it ourselves.

That keeps the heat in, the cold out.

Well, <u>some</u> of it, anyway.

5. Are there storm doors and windows in your house?

No, they're all on the outside.

Discuss these things with your parents. They will listen closely to what you say because it means saving money as well as energy.

# Solar Cells

Solar energy has a wonderful future!

Its past was no slouch, either.

...wonderful solar...
...wonderful future...
...wonderful energy...

One of the most unusual tricks is something called a solar cell. Usually the size of a silver dollar, a solar cell can be as small as the head of a pin.

Must pick up a lot of sunlight on a surface that big.

You may have seen photographs of solar cells and not even known you were looking at them. Remember seeing a photograph of a space satellite? It had large, wing-like panels coming out of it, didn't it?

You may have thought those panels helped the satellite to "fly."

No, the one I saw had small leg-like things all over it.

Watch it!

Click!

I didn't see any panels, remember?

COLOR PHOTOS OF DOG FOOD

Well, in a way, you were right.

Thanks for listening to me, Mrs. Robinson. Most teachers aren't that responsive.

But it's not the way you think. Those "wings" hold solar cells in them and when the light strikes those cells, the special material they are made of changes the light to electricity, needed to power all the electrical equipment on the satellite.

So you're back on those wings again, are you?

The special material is called photovoltaic (*foe-toe-vol-TAY-ik*) . . .

material, and that's where the big news of solar energy will be coming from in *your* lifetime! Photovoltaic solar cells can convert light into electricity.

Imagine this . . . the roof of your house covered with tiny solar cells. That would mean *all* the electricity you might need (stored in batteries) would come right from your roof.

You could cut the wires that hook you up to the nearest electric company; you wouldn't need their power anymore because your house would produce its own.

In fact, you could even sell power back to the electric company during the times when your rooftop solar cells produce more power than you need.

Now you know that solar cells are already in use in satellites' "wings"; they are being used everywhere in the world where there is no electrical wiring for small projects.

You've probably seen solar cells along the highway, powering emergency telephones. Look at your pocket calculator—it may be powered by solar cells. Photovoltaics are already being used to cook with, for light, to work the vacuum cleaner, to warm every room in the house.

So why don't we have them everywhere today?

With oil, coal, and electricity costing so much, wouldn't it be great if everyone could use solar cells to solve a good part of the energy problem?

I'll say! Where do I sign?
Put me down for 200 of them.

COOL!

Solar cells are presently undergoing experiments and improvements in their technology in business and government laboratories. In fact, the most promising new idea is "thin-film" solar cells on sheets of plastic.

One of the biggest problems with today's solar cells and the thin-film solar cells is that they can only convert about 20% of light into electricity.

Until they can be made more efficient than that, their price will often be higher than traditional energy sources.

Soon solar cells will be mass produced, which will help make them cheaper to buy. They will work much better than they do now, and you will be able to use them to make your own electricity.

Isn't that exciting?

Actually, all three types of solar power systems . . . active, passive and solar cells . . . will be combined to make houses, schools, hospitals, museums, concert halls, and businesses warm and comfortable.

It will be done at small cost, thanks to the sun. It will be done with little pollution, thanks to the sun. And one of our biggest problems . . . energy . . . will be partly solved, thanks to the sun.

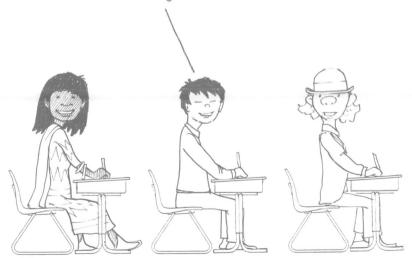

Municipal buildings, airport terminals, and army barracks will just have to make out with high-priced oil.

"Thanks to the son.
Thanks to the son.
Thanks to the son."
We daughters never
get any credit, do we?

Wait a minute. What's this, the last class? Well, Mrs. Robinson, you really outdid yourself, and I congratulate you. But before you go, how about showing me a few experiments I can do—things to keep me off the streets and out of trouble?

# Energy Experiments

— Thanks.

## Demonstrate Burning Gases

Light a candle, let is burn a few moments, and then blow it out. Quickly bring a lighted match close to the wick, but do not touch it. The flame will appear to "jump" to the wick from your lighted match. The flame is not really jumping—it is igniting the *hot gases* that are still rising from the wick.

More than any other thing you've told me, this experiment has proved to me that solar heating is a practical solution to today's energy problems.

## Demonstrate Pollution from Combustion

Hold a lighted candle under a clean piece of glass. The spot that forms on the underside of the glass can then be wiped with a tissue.

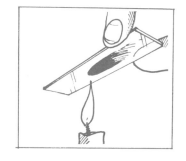

The dirt (carbon) on the tissue can be circulated in class to show pollution given off by the flame.

The thumb and forefinger can be circulated to show the principles of meat roasting.

## Demonstrate the Effect of No Sun

Use two small, potted plants. Put one in a small, light-tight box (a shoebox is fine) and the other beside it, open to the sun on a windowsill. Water them equally, as necessary. Note the progressive deterioration of the sunless plant over a period of weeks.

Make air holes in the box.

I'd wilt, too, if I had to smell shoes for that long.

## Demonstrate Heating of Absorbed Sunlight vs. Reflected Sunlight

Paint a small piece of wood (a ruler is fine) with flat black paint. Wrap about half of it with aluminum foil. Place it in the sun for an hour or so. Have students feel the temperature difference between the *absorbing* surface and the *reflecting* surface.

Why in the world would you want to heat <u>any</u> kind of sunlight?

I GRADUATED

EMERGENCY AT HOME

Looks yummy.

BOBBIE

Have your father write an essay on how his favorite ruler looked before you took it, and how it looks now.

## Locating South

Using a simple compass, point various students in different directions and ask each one to locate north and south.

Why do I need a compass to point kids in different directions?

Mark their findings on the floor with chalk, and see who comes closest to your pre-determined (but hidden) mark.

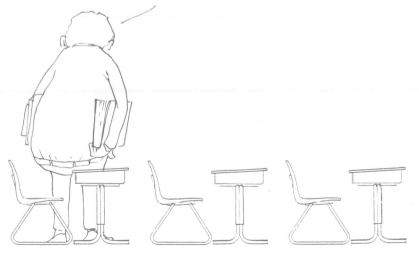

Now, how about some passive solar experiments? I want to knock a wall flat or put an oven on the roof, something like that. Got any experiments along those lines, Mrs. Robinson, or must I now be satisfied with having learned everything there is to know about solar energy? You're pointing to the door. Is that a message? OK, OK, I get it. Goodbye. See you later, Mrs. R.

# Glossary

### Active Solar System

The sun's rays heat the rooftop collector panel through which air is moving. Air at the top of the panel is hottest. Air is drawn down via ducts through blower into insulated rock bin, which absorbs much of the air's heat, allowing cooler air to rise to collector for another load of energy. When heat from rock bin is needed, simple changes in ducts allow it to enter the rooms.

### Solar Cells (PVs)

Photovoltaic panel on roof converts sunlight directly to electricity. Power is either used, stored in batteries, or sold to the power company.

## Passive Solar System

Shaded area shows Trombe wall behind insulating glass. A wall of concrete, brick, stone, or even water drums, painted black, absorbs solar heat on sunny days, and slowly radiates heat to rooms hours later. Top and bottom vents can help circulation of solar-heated air. Flaps on vents prevent unwanted reverse airflow on cold nights.

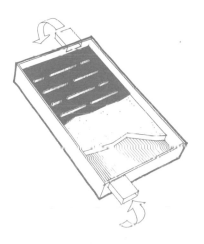

## Solar Collector

A rooftop collector, usually made of metal, has a glass or plastic cover through which solar energy passes. On striking the black surface, the energy is converted to heat, which is drawn away by the moving air. Note arrows showing how air enters and leaves, baffles to improve the transfer of heat to the air, and the insulation behind the black collector surface. Many collectors use water instead of air to carry away the heat, but the general principles are the same.

# Index